SILK AND SPICE ROUTES

Inventions
and trade

STRUAN REID

NEW YORK
UNESCO Publishing

UNESCO

Foreword

The story is told how Xiling Shi, while strolling one day in the garden, casually plucked a white cocoon from the leaf of a mulberry tree under which she was passing. She later chanced to drop the cocoon in a bowl of steaming tea and, in attempting to retrieve it, found herself unraveling a long white thread. Xiling Shi was the wife of Huangdi, the semimythical emperor who ruled China nearly 5,000 years ago; and it was in this way, according to legend, that she discovered the secret of what was to become one of China's most valuable and distinctive products—silk.

Silk was in fact only one of many precious goods exchanged between East and West along what later came to be known as the Silk Roads. Jade and lapis lazuli were carried along these routes, as were spices, fruits, and flowers such as ginger, pomegranates, and roses. Some of our basic technologies like printing and papermaking were also transmitted along these ancient arteries. Ambassadors, scholars, craftsmen, entertainers, monks, pilgrims, and soldiers all journeyed along the Silk Roads, acquiring and spreading knowledge as they went.

UNESCO is the United Nations agency responsible for promoting cooperation and understanding among nations in the areas of education, science, culture, and communication. One of its current projects is the "Integral Study of the Silk Roads: Roads of Dialogue," which seeks to explore and highlight the rich cultural exchanges and contacts that took place along the ancient Silk Roads. As part of this project, UNESCO has organized a series of expeditions over land and sea, retracing with international teams of scholars, filmmakers, photographers, and writers the journeys of those who traveled these routes through the ages.

I am sure you will enjoy reading this book in *The Silk and Spice Routes* series, copublished by UNESCO and New Discovery Books. I hope that your new knowledge about these fascinating channels of trade and communication will enable you to better understand some aspects of cultures different from your own. You will in this way—unwittingly as Xiling Shi when she discovered silk—be adding your own personal thread to that precious web of understanding between members of the human family on which the future of our planet depends.

Federico Mayor
The Director-General
UNESCO

Contents

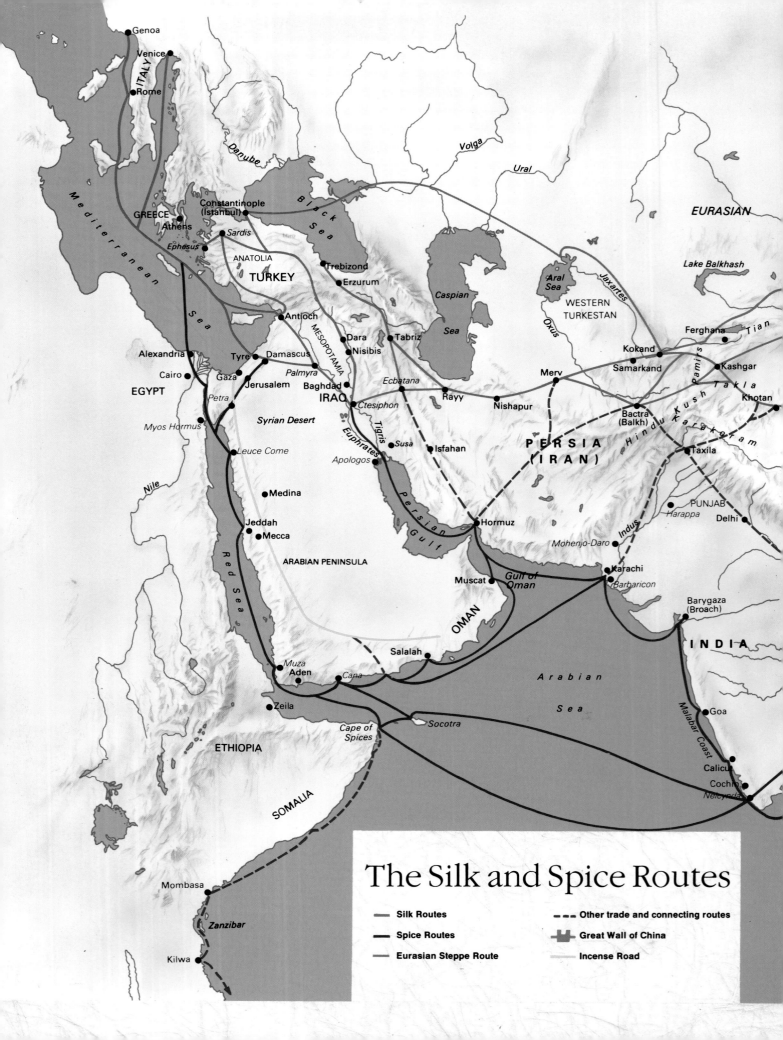

The Silk and Spice Routes

⎯⎯	Silk Routes	┅┅	Other trade and connecting routes
⎯⎯	Spice Routes	⊞⊞	Great Wall of China
⎯⎯	Eurasian Steppe Route	⎯⎯	Incense Road

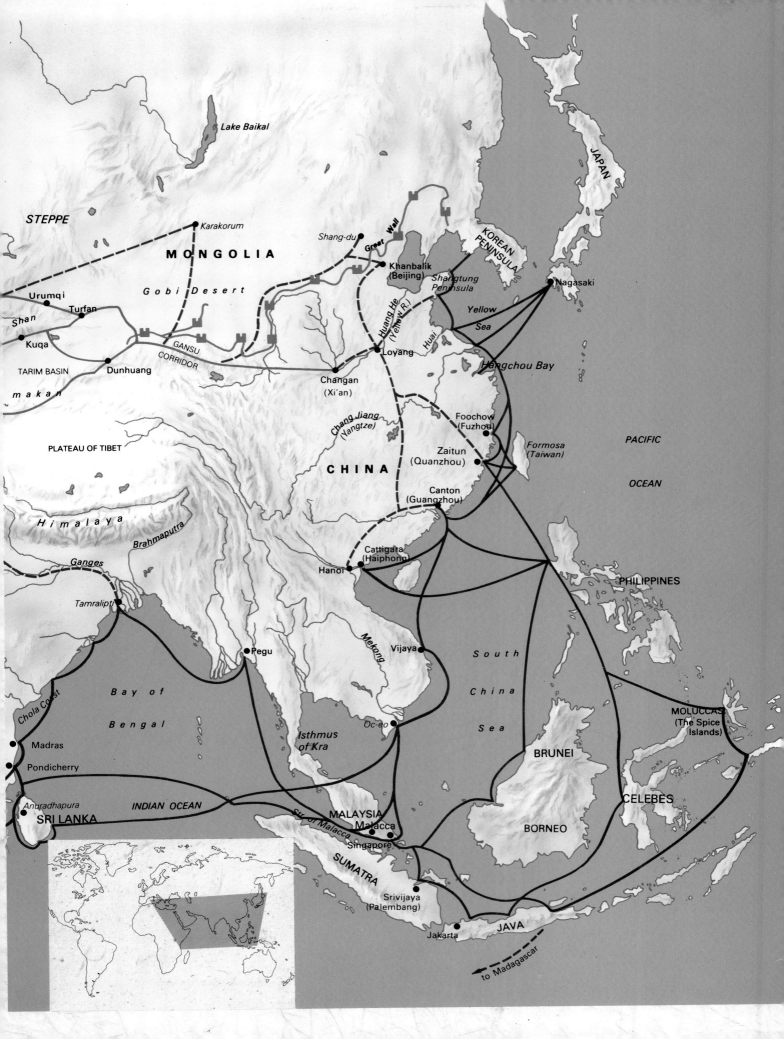

chapter one

The Paths of Innovation

An Exchange of Riches

▼ *Ships old and new still travel the Spice Routes. A modern Omani containership enters the port of Muttrah, where a traditional Arab dhow is already anchored. Many technological advances in ship-building and navigation were made through trading links.*

Over many centuries, the Silk and Spice Routes, two of the greatest trade routes in our history, wound their way across Asia, linking its people and those of Europe in a network of paths and highways, cities, towns, and ports. Kingdoms and empires rose and grew fat from the proceeds of the rich trade that passed back and forth along the routes. Some of these civilizations lasted for many hundreds of years, while others held only momentary glory, soon extinguished by a more powerful people eager to wrest the trade from their control.

The Silk Route crossed Asia by land, its paths stretching over some 5,000 miles. Starting from the ancient Chinese capital of Changan (modern Xi'an), it made its way northwest along the length of the Great Wall of China, dividing into two to skirt the Takla Makan Desert and using several high passes to cross the snow-covered peaks of the Pamir Mountains, one of the mountain ranges in central Asia that form the "Roof of the World." Travelers then moved through the lands of Afghanistan and Iran and on to the Mediterranean Sea. The valuable goods were then transferred to ships bound for Europe.

▶ *A view of the Moluccas island of Tidore seen from Ternate. The Moluccas or Spice Islands were the only source of cloves and nutmeg until the 18th century.*

The sea-lanes that made up the Spice Routes spread out around Asia over a distance of 9,000 miles. Their focal point was the famed Spice Islands, the string of Indonesian islands known today as the Moluccas, the only place where the sought-after pungent cloves and nutmegs grew. From here the Spice Routes fanned out over the China seas to China and Japan and westward to India and beyond. To reach Europe and the Mediterranean, the merchandise was carried up the Persian Gulf or the Red Sea and overland via cities such as Petra, Palmyra, and Alexandria.

The convoys of ships and the camel caravans were piled high with the luxuries of the East that were so much in demand in the cities farther west: not only spices and silks, but perfumed woods, rare animals and plants, and ivory. These were exchanged for Western goods such as lengths of cotton and woolen cloth, coral, amber, gold, and silver.

However, rare and exotic goods were not the only items to be carried up and down the Silk and Spice Routes. The routes also acted as paths for the exchange of knowledge: ideas on new technology and scientific skills, languages, art, and religion. Some of the most fundamental technologies—among them writing, weaving, agriculture, and riding skills—evolved and developed in this way. This book looks at the part that the trade of the Silk and Spice Routes played in spreading information on science, technology, and inventions all over the world.

▲ Rare and prized objects were traded across great distances from the earliest times. This necklace found in Wiltshire, England, dates from 1750–1500 B.C. It is made from amber brought from the Baltic. Amber was also traded eastward from there deep into Asia.

◀ Part of the Pala d'Oro in the Basilica of St. Mark's, Venice, begun in 1005. From the 12th–16th centuries, the city-states of Venice and Genoa became extremely rich because they had a virtual monopoly in the trade coming into Europe from the Silk and Spice Routes.

Technology, Civilization, and Empire

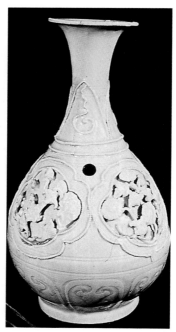

▲ *The Ptolemy cameo dates to 278 B.C. It shows the head of Alexander the Great and his Bactrian queen, Roxana. From 336–323 B.C., Alexander conquered most of western Asia, leading to a great exchange of ideas between Greek, Persian, and Indian cultures.*

▲ *14th-century porcelain vase produced in China during the Mongol Yuan dynasty (1264–1368). The Mongols controlled most of the rest of Asia at this time and trade flourished. Significantly, this vase is the first piece of porcelain on record to reach Europe.*

Technology is the tool of civilization and, in turn, technological advances contributed to the growth of civilization and the empires that went with it. The discovery and increasing use of iron demonstrates this process. Iron smelting first developed in Asia Minor about 1500 B.C. and the knowledge spread from there from about 1200 B.C. When agricultural implements such as hoes and plows, as well as weapons, could be made of iron, the effect on the society and economy of the region was enormous. With the increase in agricultural productivity came a surplus of food that led to economic development and state-building. Trade increased, resulting in a greater demand for the craftsmen needed to produce the goods for the trade. The new iron tools also made it possible to build bigger and better ships, which in their turn enabled longer sea journeys to be made and increased trade and colonization.

With this growth in trade and technology there came a need for political reorganization. Local tribal chiefs and their clans were replaced by kingdoms and then empires. These new empires enforced law and order, which then took the process further, making possible long-distance trade by land and sea. With the thousands of merchants, soldiers, and sailors who crisscrossed their way through Asia and Europe came a constant exchange of scientific and technological ideas, innovations, and inventions.

It was the existence of three strong empires in about 100 B.C. that finally enabled a land route, the Silk Route, to operate effectively across Asia: the Roman Empire in the West, the Chinese Empire of the Han dynasty (202 B.C.–A.D. 220) in the East, with the Parthian Empire in Persia (Iran, c. 247 B.C.–A.D. 224) between the two. All three were looking to expand their interests both politically and commercially and, having done so, had the power to administer and maintain them. The Romans, too, encouraged the Spice Route trade from the Red Sea to India in an attempt to bypass the Parthians. The Romans and Parthians were longtime rivals for power in western Asia, so both were reluctant to give each other the profits that resulted from trade.

Conflict and competition such as this between empires and kingdoms, cities and towns set the pattern of trade and communications along the Silk and Spice Routes throughout their history. In times of war or political uncertainty, fewer people would risk the dangers of travel over any great distance. The collapse of the Han dynasty in A.D. 220 led for a while to a virtual halt in trade between China and the West. In general, the stronger the empire, the better the communications and the greater the exchange of information. However, these elements are interlinked. The success of one contributes to and feeds off the growth of the others. At times, it is almost impossible to separate them out into cause and effect.

► Ruins of Persepolis in Iran, capital of the ancient Persian Empire of the Achaemenid dynasty. The Achaemenids ruled from 550–330 B.C., excelling in the technology of engineering and warfare, which helped them to maintain their large empire.

▲ A stone column, engraved with one of the first written codes of laws, the Code of Hammurabi, king of Babylonia (c. 1792–1750 B.C.)

chapter two

The Necessities of Trade

Overland Travel

▲ *3rd-century A.D. Persian silver gilt dish. It shows a scene of a man hunting on horseback. The horse's tack, including its reins and stirrup, is carefully depicted.*

The establishment of overland trade routes was, of course, dependent on people's ability to travel long distances and to carry a reasonable quantity of trade goods with them. The different types of countryside —hills, mountains, rivers, and vegetation—all influenced the types of routes chosen, but it was animals, such as horses and camels, that really opened up the opportunities for people to travel longer distances and over longer periods. Until the railroads of the 20th century, this was the means that enabled large-scale overland trade to take place.

The type of transport varied along the Silk Route, with merchants using either ox- or horse-drawn carts, camels, pack asses, or pack horses, depending on the land being crossed—different animals were better suited to different terrains. The merchant might ride on a horse or a donkey, but he often walked beside the animals carrying the goods. The merchandise rarely traveled from one end of its journey to the other with the same traders, and never with the same pack animals. Usually goods changed hands a number of times along the way.

The domestication of the Bactrian camel took place in the second millennium B.C. at the hands of the nomads of central Asia. The Arabian camel was domesticated at about the same time. Both types, the

▼ *Mongol nomads rounding up their horses. This is a modern continuation of their ancient traditions of breeding and riding horses.*

Bactrian camel with two humps and the Arabian with one, have an amazing capability, vital for desert travel, of going for days without water. They need little food and carry much heavier loads than horses over distances of 20 miles a day.

The horse has long been an important means of transport and was the animal most frequently used from one end of the Silk Route to the other. Throughout the third millennium B.C., the nomads of central Asia had been breeding larger and stronger horses. The larger horses made riding possible. This skill was extremely useful, particularly in battle, and was gradually acquired across Asia.

▼ *For heavy loads, stronger animals, such as these bullocks pulling carts in Mongolia, were used along sections of the Silk Route.*

◄ *Camels were not just used as pack animals. This stone relief shows an Arab in battle mounted on a camel. He is being pursued by the Assyrian cavalry on horseback.*

Improvements in the techniques of controlling the animals followed, especially the introduction of the foot stirrup and a harness with breast and collar straps. These revolutionized the transportation of people and goods. Both appeared first in China, although the stirrup may have had its origins in central Asia, where leather or rope straps were often used to assist in mounting horses. The use of stirrups gradually spread westward across central Asia and Afghanistan, and was introduced to Europe in the sixth century A.D. by the Avars of the Eurasian Steppe. The stirrup gave the Avar cavalry the upper hand in its battles with the forces of the Byzantine Empire. The Byzantine cavalry had to be completely reorganized as a result and later adopted the stirrup itself.

Sea
Transport

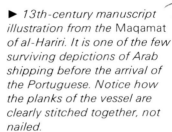

▶ *13th-century manuscript illustration from the* Maqamat *of al-Hariri. It is one of the few surviving depictions of Arab shipping before the arrival of the Portuguese. Notice how the planks of the vessel are clearly stitched together, not nailed.*

Across mountain and desert, the camel and horse could hardly be bettered as a means of transport. By contrast, there was always room for improvement in the ships that traveled the Spice Routes. Developments in ship design and construction methods came about in response to challenges encountered in trading ever farther afield. Observations made and information exchanged on these journeys also brought practical knowledge. So the expansion of trade by sea was closely bound up with the evolution of shipping and navigation.

Some of the Spice Routes had been in operation from as early as

2000 B.C. and the Romans had established them as an effective rival to the Silk Route for the passage of East-West trade. But it was under the Arabs and Omanis from the seventh century onward that the sea routes really came into their own. The Arabs quickly recognized the importance of sea power in defending their new and rapidly expanding Islamic empire. But they also came to see the great advantages that sea transport gave them in trading their products and earning them wealth as the predominant sea carriers between East and West.

With their conquest of Syria (part of the Byzantine Empire) in the seventh century, the Arabs employed Syrian and Greek shipwrights to build them a powerful Mediterranean war fleet. Farther east, a second war fleet was built for the Arabs by Persian shipwrights. All the ships and boats were carvel-built, that is, the planks of the hulls were laid edge to edge, not overlapping as they were in clinker-built ships common in northern Europe. But the ships of the Western Fleet followed the Greek and Syrian technical traditions, with the planks nailed to an internal framework. The ships of the Eastern Fleet, however, were built according to Persian and Indian practice, with the hull planking "sewn" together with palm-fiber twine, which was cheaper and more easily available than iron nails.

It was in the Indian Ocean that the triangular lateen sail first appeared, and the Arabs introduced it from there to the Mediterranean sometime during the seventh or eighth centuries. The lateen sail, although not easy to handle, enables a ship to sail much closer to the wind and so take more direct and quicker routes. The Portuguese caravel, in which they made the first European journeys around Africa to India, was similar in design to the Arab *baghla*, with lateen sails and carvel (caravel) planking for the hull.

Until the arrival of the Portuguese in the Indian Ocean at the end of the 15th century, little change took place in the design of ships in the area. However, the competition from the Portuguese boats led the Arabs and Omanis to substitute the stronger nailing for sewing in the construction of their ships. A square-sterned European design was also introduced in place of the sharp two-ended stern previously characteristic of Persian Gulf and Indian Ocean shipping.

◄ *The* Zinat al Bihaar, *a recently built Omani* baghla *belonging to the sultan of Oman. The decorated stern of the ship is following a tradition introduced into the Indian Ocean by the Portuguese.*

▲ *An Arab boatbuilder works on the construction of a dhow, a smaller sailing boat still used throughout the Indian Ocean.*

▲ *This illustration from the 15th-century* Livre des Merveilles *is the first to show a compass in use in European shipping.*

Finding the Way

Even the most experienced sailors frequently found themselves off course. Storms, shipwrecks, and strange and often hostile lands were hazards common to all seafarers. Finding the way became easier as the larger and better-designed ships sailed farther. Sailors brought back practical knowledge, as well as trade goods, which led to more detailed mapping of the oceans and coasts and improvements in the design of navigational instruments.

Once again, the Muslim sailors of Persia, Arabia, and Oman added a great deal of knowledge to world geography, which they passed on to the Europeans. In particular, there was a lot of exchange of Islamic expertise in drawing up nautical charts, known as portolans. These were very important tools for the mariner as they gave wind directions and bearings needed to sail from port to port.

In the mid-12th century, detailed information on India, China, and North Africa was passed to the Europeans through the patronage of two kings of Sicily—Roger II (1127–1154) and his son William I (1154–1166). With their backing, an Arab scholar from Morocco named al-Idrisi (1100–1166) produced a complete description of the world as then known to the Muslims. This information was set out in a series of 70 maps with a written description in a volume known as the *Kitab al-rujari* (The Book of Roger).

▲ *A Chinese geomancer's compass used to make sure a building faced in a direction favorable to good luck. The navigational compass developed from this earlier use.*

▶ *Page from a portolan atlas c. 1650 showing the Arabian Peninsula and the eastern Mediterranean.*

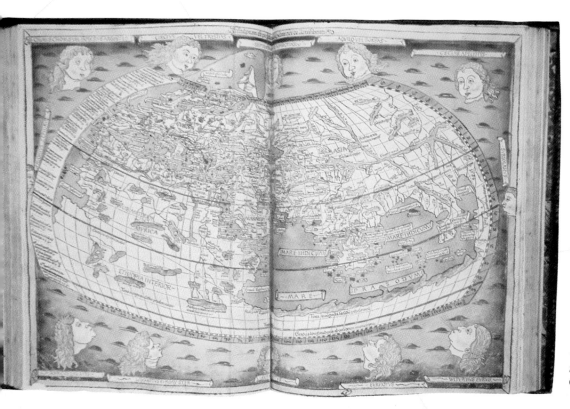

◄ *A map of the world dating to 1486, based on Ptolemy's* Geography.

Al-Idrisi's knowledge and that of earlier Arab geographers was partly based upon Persian-Sasanian, Indian, and Greek sources. The influence of Sasanian geographical knowledge can be seen in many areas, such as the name for the Indian Ocean, which the Arabs called *bahr al-fars* (the Persian Sea) following Sasanian examples. Indian and Greek geographical works were translated into Arabic, including those of the Graeco-Egyptian geographer, astronomer, and mathematician Claudius Ptolemy (c. A.D. 90–170). His monumental work, the *Geography,* was an early attempt to map the known world and provided the basis for much later Arabic cartography.

▲ *One of the maps from the* Kitab al-rujari *(The Book of Roger).*

In the area of navigational instruments, the introduction of the mariner's compass to western Asia and Europe at the beginning of the 13th century marked a significant stage, for the first time permitting accurate directions for navigation. The magnetic compass had existed in China for a number of centuries before, but it was only late in its history that it came to be used for navigation at sea, sometime between 850 and 1050. The Chinese were active in the Spice Route trade, although their junks were often sailed by Koreans, and the compass seems to have reached Islam and Europe at about the same time through nautical contact with China. The first mention of a compass in European writings occurred in 1190 and in Arabic writings about 1232.

Recording
Information

► *Engraving depicting a Dutch printing office in the late 16th century. It shows the various stages involved in printing a book, including the arrangement of the movable type.*

▲ *8th-century wall painting from a cave temple on the Silk Route to the west of Turfan. It shows a Buddhist scribe at work.*

Among the most important inventions in the history of civilization has been the art of writing, for it has enabled people to make permanent records of their achievements and culture. It is also an important tool of trade: commercial transactions can be recorded, along with taxes on goods and produce. Indeed, it seems it was largely for this purpose that writing systems were developed in the first place.

This development occurred in about 3000 B.C. among the Sumerians of Mesopotamia, now part of Iraq. It consisted of simplified pictures of objects, called pictographs. Independently, about a thousand years later, the Chinese also started to use a form of pictographs (characters) that is still the basis of the script they use today. However, in the West, a further innovation occurred around 1000 B.C., when the Phoenicians developed an alphabet. The Phoenicians, from what is now Lebanon, had an extensive trading empire around the Mediterranean. Probably as a result of their trading contacts, their alphabet became the foundation of many scripts still in use today. In Europe, the Greek and subsequently our Roman alphabet evolved from it. In Asia, it gave rise, through a script called Aramaic, to the Arabic, Hebrew, and Indian Brahmi writing systems.

Scripts were written on a variety of different surfaces but it was in China, in the second century B.C., that paper was invented. The Chinese kept the secret until 751, when the Arabs acquired the knowledge of papermaking from some Chinese captured at the battle of Talas River in central Asia. Soon Samarkand and Baghdad had important paper industries. For 500 years, the Arabs, in turn, jealously guarded their secret from the Europeans, though they happily sold them paper at great profit. The first manufacture of paper in Europe was in the 12th century in Spain, then under Muslim rule, but it was not until the following century that a paper industry was in full operation in Italy.

The invention and manufacture of paper directly paved the way for the invention of printing. Printing from blocks of wood on to paper first occurred in China in the seventh century A.D. Buddhist monks were largely responsible for this as they needed many more copies of their sacred texts than copiers could produce. The earliest known printed book is the Buddhist *Diamond Sutra*, produced in 868.

▲ *A page from a 10th-century copy of the Koran, Islam's most sacred text. It is written on paper, by then widely available in western Asia.*

◄ *Two Buddhist monks using woodblocks to print religious texts in a monastery in the Everest region of Nepal. It is probably for this purpose that printing first developed in China.*

Korea was the first country to which printing spread from China, around 700. From there it was introduced by Buddhist monks to Japan. In the mid-11th century, printing by movable type also originated in China. Movable wooden type dating from about 1300 has been found in the city of Turfan in Sinkiang. It was introduced there from China following the Mongol conquest of the region. The Mongol armies passed on farther westward, overrunning Russia, Poland, and Hungary from 1240 to 1242. It is possible that before he invented movable type in Germany in 1455, Johann Gutenberg had heard about its use farther eastward.

Weighing and
Paying

If a record of trade was needed, so, too, was a method of describing the quantities bought and sold. The development of systems for measurement went hand in hand with the development of writing. The earliest use of balances was probably for the weighing of gold dust. This commodity was so precious that it needed very careful and accurate measurement. Because of the limitations of weighing gold, only small units were at first needed. The standard unit of weight was the shekel, which was used throughout the Middle East, ranging in weight from 7.78 to 14.3 grams. When larger weights were needed, the mina (25 to 100 shekels) was introduced and later the talent (weighing 60 minas).

▲ This is an early example of a Chinese banknote. The Chinese were the first to use paper money, in the 11th century.

▶ Greek plate of the 6th century B.C. The scene depicted shows balance scales being used to weigh silphium, a substance valued for its medicinal properties.

▶▶ From its origins around the eastern Mediterranean, the use of the coin spread along the trade routes. This bronze coin of the 1st century A.D. was minted in the Kushan kingdom of central Asia. It appropriately features a Bactrian camel.

As early as 1350 B.C., Egyptian balances could weigh a shekel of gold to within an accuracy of 1 percent. They were of the basic modern design, with a beam pivoted at the center and carrying the object to be weighed at one end and weights at the other. The Roman steelyard, which is still used today, was a different type of balance in which the object being weighed was counterbalanced not by changing a weight at the other end of the arm, but by moving a fixed weight along the arm.

These balances and similar ones were used by traders in towns and ports up and down the Silk and Spice Routes. At first, goods and services would have been exchanged by barter, swapping one item for another. Types of items being exchanged were developed into forms of currency, such as measures of grain, lengths of silk, or, more commonly, bars of metal, such as copper. In many societies, small amounts of metals were used as a medium of exchange as they were long-lasting, could be carried easily, and could be seen to have a value according to their size and purity. The importance of weight in early currencies is preserved today in such words as "pound," "lira," and "ruble," all units of weight.

◄ Gold coin minted around 1st–2nd centuries A.D. by the Kushan king Wima-kadphises. The Kushans controlled a large empire in central Asia from 1st–3rd centuries and greatly encouraged trade on the Silk Route.

▼ A superb bronze weight in the form of a human bust, attached to a Roman steelyard scales.

Sometime in the eighth century B.C., the Lydians of western Asia Minor (modern Turkey) began stamping pieces of metal and guaranteeing their quality and weight. The use of coins quickly spread among the Greek merchants of Ionia who traded along the coast of Asia Minor. They, in turn, brought the idea to mainland Greece, where the technique of stamping flat, circular, and two-sided coins developed. Gold and silver coins now helped interregional trade while other, less valuable copper coins enabled farmers to sell their produce rather than barter it. This led to a greater flexibility within trading networks, increasing efficiency and productivity all around. Eventually, gold and silver coins were used throughout the trade routes.

Later, the use of paper money, first developed in China in the 11th century A.D., was adopted by the Mongols after their conquest of China in 1264. They introduced the idea throughout their massive empire, including the lands of central Asia and Iran.

chapter three

The Maintenance of Empire

Keeping the Road Open

▲ *16th-century Mogul manuscript illustration showing the Red Fort in Agra, India, being built*

▲ *Detail from the Emperor Trajan's Column in Rome. It shows a bridge built over the Danube by the Roman armies during the period when Trajan (A.D. 53–117) extended the Roman Empire into the regions north of that river.*

With the rise and expansion of empires, there was a need to administer and police them efficiently. Fast lanes of communication were essential in order to control these huge territories. The formidable empire of Cyrus the Great of Persia (559–530 B.C.) had the earliest network of highways. The so-called Royal Road ran 1,700 miles from Susa near the north of the Persian Gulf westward to the Tigris and then across Syria to Ephesus on the Aegean coast. All along the way, it was serviced with inns and relay stations. These roads were not really designed for merchants and travelers but were mainly military and administrative highways. However, their existence inevitably helped the growth of trade.

The Chinese built an elaborate system of highways and canals that, as well as transporting goods, were important for the administration of the empire. Later, the Mongols used these and the Silk Route generally to administer their empire, with an efficient messenger service running between the cities and caravansaries (roadside inns) along its paths. The highway system constructed by the Romans across their vast empire was so well made that many stretches still exist today and formed the basis of Europe's and the Middle East's modern highway system. Their network of splendid roads extended over some 50,000 miles.

In other areas of civil and mechanical engineering, Roman skills lay in the construction of huge public buildings such as amphitheaters, baths, basilicas, bridges, and aqueducts. They built complex fortifications and ports, vital for protecting their communications and trade. Their use of concrete from the second century B.C. enabled them to build stronger and bigger buildings than before. They developed the use of the arch, the vault, and the dome, which enabled them to span ever greater areas.

Via the Byzantine Empire (the name given to the eastern Roman Empire from 610), the Arabs inherited many of the Roman methods of construction in their Islamic empire, combining them with knowledge gained from their Iranian territories. In later centuries as their military architecture developed, especially during the Crusades from the 11th to 13th centuries, there was much cross-fertilization between Islam, Byzantium, and the West. Ideas passed from one region to another as improvements in siege techniques called for matching improvement in defenses. Paradoxically, technological exchanges took place in the very areas where Islam and Christianity confronted each other. For example, the Islamic development of a "machicolation" gallery projecting over the gateway, with holes in its floor through which boiling oil could be poured on to the heads of attackers, was used much later in castles as far west as Ireland.

◄ View of the Crusader castle of Krak des Chevaliers in Syria, built during the 12th–13th centuries. The Crusaders adopted many of the Arabic ideas for fortified buildings.

Arms and Warfare

Military architecture needed to become ever more sophisticated to withstand the use of more powerful weapons. People have always been remarkably inventive when it comes to developing new weapons. There has always been a need for an advantage over enemy forces, to kill more people at greater distances.

▲ *Bronze sculpture of a Parthian bowman using a composite bow. He has just fired one arrow and is pulling out another from his quiver.*

▶ *Illustration from a 16th-century manuscript showing cannon being used by the Ottoman army during their siege of a Hungarian fort*

The history of gunpowder clearly illustrates the exchange of ideas in arms and warfare that took place by means of the trade routes. Gunpowder was first invented by the Chinese in the 9th century A.D., not as a weapon but as an elixir of immortality. The first use of gunpowder in warfare occurs in 919 when it was used as a fuse for the ignition of a Chinese flamethrower. Gunpowder made possible the later invention of guns and cannons. The gun proper was eventually developed in China sometime during the 13th century—a bronze handgun dating from 1288 has been excavated in northeastern China.

The spread of knowledge and use of gunpowder westward took place in a number of stages. In 1265, an English scientist and Franciscan monk named Roger Bacon (c. 1214–c. 1294) first described gunpowder being used in a type of firecracker. This information may have reached him through his friend and fellow Franciscan William of Rubrouck, who returned from a mission to the Mongol capital of Karakorum in 1256.

▲ *Illustration of a 14th-century Turkish trebuchet. This was a device for hurling heavy missiles, like a giant catapult. Its use was adopted throughout Europe.*

Many foreigners were welcomed and employed at the courts of the Mongol emperors. Knowledge of devices such as cannons, bombs, grenades, and rockets may have reached Europe through merchants like Marco Polo, while Muslim military experts took service under the Mongols specifically to learn Eastern methods of warfare. In 1340, cannons were used by the Muslims at the battle of Tarif in Spain. The first battle in northern Europe in which cannons are reported to have been used was Crécy in northern France in 1346.

There were great advances in gunpowder technology in Europe during the 15th century and a number of European adaptations of Chinese weapons were exported back to China. For example, the Portuguese culverin, a development of the Chinese breechloader, reached China by about 1510. In a similar way, the serpentine may originally have been a Chinese invention. It was developed into the matchlock musket or arquebus either by the Turks or the Europeans. The Chinese probably saw it again in its new form in about 1520, introduced by the people of central Asia.

The design of many other weapons throughout history has followed this same pattern of give-and-take. For example, a powerful missile-thrower called a trebuchet entered the Islamic armory from China by way of central Asia toward the end of the seventh century. Similarly, the extremely powerful composite bow, invented by the nomads of central Asia, became part of the armory of both the Chinese and Persian armies. They also adopted later innovations made to the bow by the nomads.

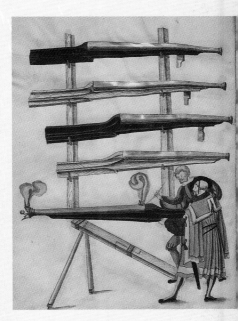

▲ *Illustration of a collection of arquebuses, one at the bottom being demonstrated. It comes from a 16th-century work called* The Book of Arms.

chapter four

Producing the Goods

Food for All

However safe the routes the merchants traveled, trade would have been impossible without the goods to sell. On both a local and international scale, farming produce, that is, food, formed a core part of the trade and alongside this there was exchange in agricultural knowledge and techniques. By way of the trade routes, China gained new crops, such as grapes, cucumbers, and tea, while to the West came rice, pears, and even roses.

The dry climatic conditions of many parts of Asia have always demanded every conceivable means of making the maximum use of the available water. This is particularly true of much of the Islamic world and water irrigation is one of the most developed technologies in the whole of Muslim civilization. In this, the Muslims were heirs to the experience and techniques of the Sasanians, ancient Egyptians, and Romans. Ancient methods of raising, storing, and distributing water were developed and extended by the Muslims; old irrigation systems were repaired and new ones built. They made use of the ancient *qanat* system, still in use today in Iran, Syria, Oman, and the Sinkiang region of western China. This is an extremely sophisticated underground canal system, which avoids evaporation by bringing water from high up in the mountains down to towns lying in the desert that have no water systems of their own. It originated in Iran but its use spread both east and west from there. Many of the Silk Route towns on the edges of the Takla Makan Desert could not have existed without it.

▲ *Illustration from a 13th-century Persian manuscript. Cattle turn a wheel that works a mechanism to extract water from the ground. People gather around the pool where the water pours out.*

▶ *A Chinese farm laborer plowing a field, from a Chinese farming manual of the 17th century. A number of features from the Chinese plow were later adopted by the Europeans.*

◀ *Page from a Persian book on agriculture, dating to 1199. It shows various agricultural scenes, including plants being harvested and grain being winnowed.*

Later, in the 17th century, a great deal of technological information on China and Southeast Asia, including farm tools and agricultural books, was brought back to Europe by merchants and scientists. Of particular importance in this area were the Christian Jesuit missionaries who established their first mission in Beijing at this time. The Jesuits were keen observers of many things, apart from religion, and were scientifically trained, some in astronomy and others in engineering, botany, and agriculture. They sent back much information on a wide range of subjects to European countries, including a series of albums illustrating Chinese agriculture and tea production.

This growing awareness of the farming methods and implements of the Far East inspired some of the innovations made in northern Europe during the 17th and 18th centuries in what has become known as the agricultural revolution. For example, it is very likely that the design of the modern European plow followed that of the Chinese plow, using a light wooden frame and iron to make the curved moldboard. It was this tool that did so much to transform farming and food production in northern Europe.

▼ *(right) Engraving of 1667 of a Jesuit priest called Father Adam Schall. The Jesuits were often trained in many sciences and passed much new information to the West.*

▼ *(left) Aerial view of a system of underground water channels* (qanats) *still in use in many Asian countries today. This is an ancient but very sophisticated method of irrigation.*

The Mystery of
Metals

▲ *1st-century A.D. Roman stone relief. It shows workmen shaping metal vessels in their workshop.*

Metals, whether shaped into coins, jewelry, plates, or bowls, were an important item of trade between East and West. The skills of the metalsmith were legendary and often associated with magic and alchemy (see page 38). Patiently and persistently, he learned his art by trial and error, passing on his specialized knowledge over thousands of years by example and word of mouth. He was the possessor of a mysterious knowledge that could transform dull lumps of rock into dazzling metals.

▲ *Two illustrations from* De re metallica *by Georgius Agricola (1494-1555). This was a famous work on mining and metallurgy and these two scenes show the roasting of metal ores.*

Metals occur either on their own in an uncombined state, such as gold, or in a mixture of minerals called ores. Pure metals like gold probably attracted people's attentions first because of their glitter. They can be shaped simply with a hammer and an anvil. The ancient Egyptians regarded gold as the "body of the gods" and had an insatiable appetite for it. Metals in ores, however, need to be processed in two stages. First, the metal is extracted from its ore by smelting. Second, the metal needs to be worked up into objects that can be used. Molten or liquid metal can be poured into molds and the cooled and hardened metal shape then finished by hammering.

The technology and skills needed to process metals first appeared in the Middle East at the beginning of the fourth millenium B.C. From there the knowledge of working metals spread westward to Europe and eastward to Afghanistan and then India. It is likely that it was passed on farther eastward to China and Southeast Asia. This spread east and west came about either through migrating peoples bringing with them the new skills, or through traveling metalsmiths and traders who introduced new metals and new techniques for working them. For example, during the seventh century A.D., the Sogdians, a people of central Asia heavily involved in trade, introduced to the Chinese finely wrought chain mail along with the necessary skills to produce it.

▲ *7th-century* B.C. *gold animal figurine. It was made by Scythian craftsmen, famed as skilled metalsmiths and horsemen.*

Living on the northern paths of the Silk Route, the nomadic peoples of the Eurasian Steppe had a strong tradition of working metal. Their wealth needed to be easily portable so ornaments and jewelry made of precious metal were ideal forms for it to take. The style of this metalwork reflected their knowledge and interest in animals, particularly horses, and also those civilizations with which they traded, such as the Chinese, Persian, and Greek. The Scythians, a nomadic people who occupied an area north of the Black Sea from the eighth to fourth centuries B.C., are particularly famous for the spectacular gold ornaments and implements they made. It is possible that they achieved such remarkable standards of workmanship partly through contact with Greek traders around the Black Sea.

▲ *A smithy in Iran today. Two metalsmiths are hammering the heated metal before shaping it.*

Glass and Ceramics

▲ *Engraving of a Venetian glass furnace. From* De la Pirotechnia *by Vannoccio Biringuccio, 1540. The ingredients are being heated until molten and then blown into shapes.*

▲ *Glassblowing follows the same methods today as when it was introduced in the mid-1st century B.C.*

▶ *A selection of Sogdian blown glass vessels, dating from the 8th century A.D.*

"Glass is one of the most noble things which man hath at this day for his use upon the earth." So wrote Antonio Neri, the author of the first modern book on glassmaking, published in Florence in 1612, and this opinion has been shared for thousands of years as glass was traded along the Silk and Spice Routes. For example, the glassmakers of Rome were given a special street where they could practice their art. In the Byzantine period, glassmakers were exempted from taxation. And, much later, the glass craftsmen of Venice and Altare in Italy ranked with the nobility.

Glass is made from a heated mixture of silica (usually sand, flint, or quartz) and a flux (usually potash or soda), with lime added to make the glass stronger. These ingredients are placed in crucibles in a furnace where they are heated so that they fuse and become a molten liquid. Colored glass can be made by adding metallic oxides.

Inheriting skills from Syria and Egypt, Roman glass producers created a major industry from the first century B.C., as a result of the expansion of the Roman Empire and the growth of its trade network. This was partly the result of the discovery made in the mid-first century B.C. in Syria that glass can be blown like a bubble. Before this, glass had always been molded. The new method enabled craftsmen to produce a whole range of vessels of different shapes and sizes that before had only been possible in metal and clay.

For a time following the collapse of the Roman Empire, the production of glassware in Europe went into decline. But under the Sasanian emperors of Persia (224–651), glass production improved. The objects produced in this period show great technical skill and delicacy, and some were exported as far away as Japan. The Persians passed their glassmaking skills on to the Sogdians, and it is likely they passed them still farther east. A Chinese chronicle written in the seventh century records how "the inhabitants of Yeuh Chih (central Asia), while trading in the Chinese capital, declared that they knew how to make colored glass" and describes how a hundred people in the city were taught

▲ *Panel of lusterware ceramic tiles from Iran, dating to the 13th century. The use of metallic lusters on ceramics was adopted from glassmaking.*

how to manufacture it, leading to a great reduction in prices.

China's glass production may have owed a debt to the West, but in ceramics the situation was reversed. By 900, the Chinese had produced kilns where the temperature was high enough (2,640°F) to make delicate porcelain, and they were soon exporting it to western Asia. The effect was dramatic, and Islamic potters strove to produce such high-quality ware. They did not succeed, but made other innovations instead: they developed the use of a tin glaze, which gives a good white background for painting, imitating Chinese porcelain. They also evolved the use of metallic lusters on pottery, a technique borrowed from the glassmaker. And it was the export of the blue pigment of cobalt from Iran to China in the 12th century that enabled the Chinese to produce their famous blue-and-white porcelain ware.

▲ *Early 19th-century illustration showing the collection of kaolin clay in China. It was this fine white clay that enabled the Chinese to first produce porcelain.*

Spinning and
Weaving

▲ *Nomads from Uzbekistan in central Asia proudly display one of their hand-embroidered cloths.*

Spinning fibers to produce yarn and then weaving it into cloth or carpets are basic processes that have been practiced since the very earliest times. There does not seem to have been any particular pattern in the development of the equipment used in this craft. Availability of materials, population growth and the resulting increase in demand, many different climates, and all the other factors that control the development of civilizations played their part.

Spinning is the process of drawing out and then winding or twisting the textile fibers into a continuous thread. Various types of handheld spindles for doing this were developed among ancient civilizations. However, the spinning wheel came into use as a development of the hand-spindle and represents a great step forward in textile

▶ *Illustration from the* Luttrell Psalter *of 1338. It shows the spinning and carding (combing) of wool and is the earliest European record of a spinning wheel in use.*

manufacture. It provides a good example of the movement of textile technology from East to West. It probably had its origins in China and derived from the machinery used for processing silk fibers. A single continuous strand of silk runs for several hundred feet, and the silk-weaving industry in China obviously needed a silk-winding machine that could deal with these extremely long fibers.

The silk industry was operating in China from at least the 14th century B.C., although it was probably many centuries after that

date that the spinning wheel was developed. It is possible that spinning wheels were introduced to Europe by Italian merchants and missionaries who traveled to China during the rule of the Mongol Yuan dynasty (A.D. 1280–1368). The earliest picture of a spinning wheel in Europe appears in the *Luttrell Psalter* in England, dating to 1338. But the spinning wheel may have been introduced much earlier to Europe by the Arabs during their period in Sicily and Spain. They may have taken it along with their knowledge of silk manufacture.

Weaving is the main operation in the production of textiles and is carried out on a loom. The basic principle is to interlace one set of threads (known as the warp) at right angles through another set of threads (known as the woof). The framework of the loom holds taut the lengthwise warp threads, while the crosswise woof thread is woven in.

Silk, woolen, and cotton cloth are woven in this way, with variations in technique to allow for the different qualities of threads, as are flat-woven rugs and carpets, such as the kilim. However, pile carpets are made by knotting lengths of yarn on to threads strung on a vertical loom. From the earliest times, weavers practiced their craft along the trade routes, refining their art and developing their designs, as they compared their work to the cloth and carpets brought in by foreign trade.

▶ *A Turkoman woman spinning wool on a spindle. This is the simplest and most ancient method of spinning wool into threads and is still practiced in parts of the world today.*

The Queen of Fibers

Of all the products of spinning and weaving, silk fabrics have always been regarded as the most luxurious. From the time of the Silk Route's opening around 100 B.C., silk formed the bulk of the trade exported west from China but, for several centuries to come, outside of China, its origins were shrouded in mystery, giving still greater value to the exotic cloth.

▼ Early 19th-century illustration showing the selection of silk moths for breeding. This was a very important early stage in the silk-making process and only the finest moths were chosen.

► Engraving from an 18th-century English book showing the various stages in the manufacture of silk. The silk moth cocoons are placed in hot water and the threads are then unwound.

Silk thread is made by twisting together several of the long strands of fiber produced by a silkworm (the caterpillar of a specially bred moth) when it spins its cocoon. Legend has it that the Chinese empress Xiling Shi (see Foreword on page 2) first started to raise silkworms around 2600 B.C. Sericulture, as silk manufacture is called, seems to have started around this time and for many centuries the Chinese kept the production of silk a closely guarded secret.

Once the Silk Route was open, the techniques of weaving the silken thread did begin to spread, perhaps because they were similar to those used to weave other cloth. By 300 A.D., silk cloth was being woven in central and western Asia using Chinese thread. However, at the start of the fifth century, people in Khotan, an oasis on the southern path of the Silk Route around the Takla Makan Desert, learned the secret of silk production itself. The story goes that one of its kings married a Chinese princess, who smuggled silkworms and mulberry seeds (the silkworm feeds exclusively from the mulberry tree) out of China in her headdress.

Equally underhand practices appear to have been used in the progress of the secret further west. In A.D. 552, certain Persian Christians (probably from the heretical Nestorian sect) are said to have smuggled silkworms from Khotan to the court of the Byzantine emperor Justinian I (483–565), hidden in their hollow walking canes. The authenticity of this account is hard to establish, as is the story of the Chinese princess. However, silk began to be produced in Byzantium around this time and, significantly, trading contacts with central Asia were improving.

In 568, a delegation arrived in Constantinople from the Turkish Empire, which, centered on Mongolia, had expanded west across the Eurasian Steppe as far as the Byzantine border. The aim of the Turks was to bypass Persia and establish direct trade in silk with Byzantium. A Byzantine emissary went, in turn, to visit the Turkish khan and, for a brief ten years, Europe had knowledge of central Asia and access to Chinese silk outside the control of Persian middlemen.

From then onward, sericulture gradually spread through western Asia and Europe. By the 15th century, Italy and France had become the leading European producers of silk. However, in both the manufacture of silk and the weaving of fabric, the Chinese were hard to surpass. As late as 1837, a French silk expert, Camille Beauvais, wrote of "the undeniable superiority of Chinese methods over European ones," noting that the Chinese "lose scarcely one silkworm in a hundred, whereas with us the mortality rate is well over 50 percent."

▼ *Silk threads being woven into lengths of cloth in central Asia today. Hand-operated looms are still used to make the best-quality silk, although most silk is now produced on mechanized looms.*

▲ *(above and top left, page 32) Fragments of patterned silk, dating from the 7th–8th centuries A.D., found in the caves at Dunhuang, China*

◄ *Silkworms feed on a rich diet of mulberry leaves before they spin their cocoons.*

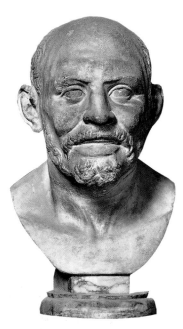

▲ *Stone bust of the Greek philosopher and astronomer Democritus (c. 460–370 B.C.). He introduced many ideas on astronomy to Greece from the Middle East and Asia.*

▲ *16th-century illustration of an observatory at Constantinople. Astronomers can be seen at work, using instruments such as astrolabes and sextants to calculate the position of the stars and planets.*

chapter five

Ways of Scientific Exchange

Observing the Skies

Technological innovation was not the only form of scientific exchange to be channeled along the Silk and Spice Routes. The more scholarly ideas and learning of many different cultures were also brought together. Ancient science was closely associated with religious and philosophical concerns and, for this reason, few scholars restricted themselves to one area of study—astronomy, astrology, mathematics, and alchemy were all closely linked.

One of the earliest sciences to emerge was astronomy. People observed the skies as a way of judging the time and season, when to plant and harvest their crops, or when to hold a religious festival. People believed that the movement of the stars in some way revealed the future, giving rise to the science of astrology. The Babylonians of Mesopotamia were probably the first people to study these two sciences. They built huge temples called ziggurats as long ago as 3000 B.C. From these temples they worshiped their gods—the Sun, the Moon, and the planet Venus. The priests carefully watched the skies and by 450 B.C. had developed the mathematics to predict the movements of the sun and planets.

The Greek astronomer-philosopher Democritus (c. 460–370 B.C.) visited Babylonia and also traveled throughout Asia Minor and Egypt. Among other learning, he introduced to Greece the Babylonian method for calculating the movement of the planets and constellations. Also using the discoveries of the Babylonians, another Greek philosopher, Thales of Miletus (c. 640–550 B.C.), was able to predict an eclipse of the sun. He also used Egyptian methods of astronomy to devise a system for navigating ships by the stars. Later Greeks tried to explain the movements of the sun, moon, and the planets. The philosopher Aristotle (384–322 B.C.) thought that they moved in perfect circles around the earth, which lay at the center of the universe, an idea later developed by Claudius Ptolemy (c. A.D. 90–170) in his book known as the *Almagest*. This work was lost to western Europe for many centuries, but it was preserved in the libraries of Constantinople and scholars from that city brought it to the attention of Western learning when the city fell to the Turks in 1453.

Trading contacts and empire-building led Indian astronomy and astrology to show strong Babylonian and Greek influences. The Indians translated into their language many Greek technical terms and principles and also methods peculiar to Greek astronomy. The signs of the zodiac that appear in Indian works are similar to those used in Greek astrological works. From the fourth century A.D., there was a steady stream of Buddhist scholars from India to China along the Silk Route. Their main job was to carry out missionary work, but they also spread more secular learning. During the seventh century, many Indian astronomical works were taught in China.

Indian astronomical knowledge, along with Greek and Persian, also played its part in Islamic astronomy and astrology. During the reign of the second caliph of the Abassid dynasty, al-Mansur (754–775), Indian astronomers brought planetary tables and texts for the calculation of eclipses to his court in Baghdad, and many Indian astronomical works were translated into Arabic.

▲ *View of the Observatory at Delhi, India, which is like an open-air planetarium. It was constructed by the maharaja of Jaipur between 1718–1724. The maharaja was a keen astronomer, following a long tradition of Indian scholarship.*

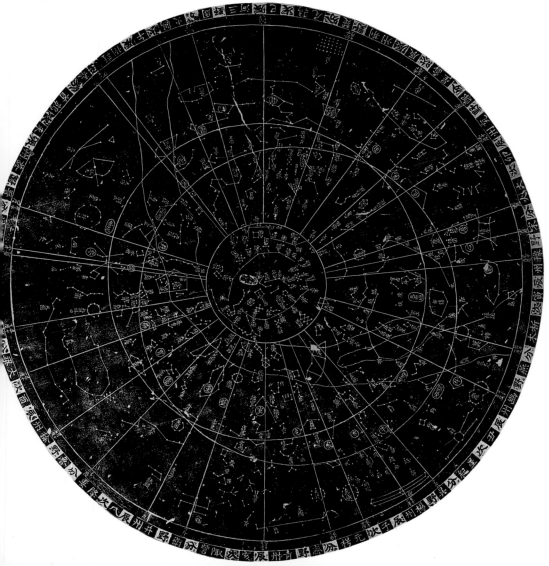

◀ *Chinese star map known as Soochow astronomical chart made c. 1193. Even though it was drawn up from observation made by the naked eye alone, the map is remarkable for its detail, showing the curving course of the Milky Way and the Crab nebula.*

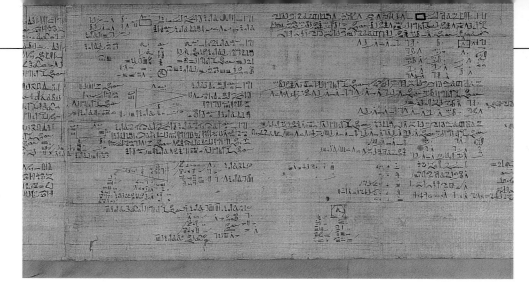

▶ *The Rhind papyrus, dating to 1800 B.C. This is one of the earliest known examples of Egyptian mathematical calculations. The Egyptian work played an important part in the foundation of Greek mathematics.*

Mathematics

▲ *A mathematics class in progress in China. Notice that alongside the Chinese script, they are working in Arabic numerals, a counting system now used throughout the world.*

▶ *The Flagellation of* Christ *by Piero della Francesca (c. 1419–1492). The picture uses a complex form of perspective, worked out with great mathematical accuracy. Piero della Francesca was one of several Renaissance artists to investigate ways of applying mathematical rules to his art, reflecting the new awareness of both science and art that occurred at this time.*

Given the close association between astronomy and mathematics, it is not surprising that the pattern of their development along the Silk and Spice Routes is much the same. Early advances were made by the Egyptians and Babylonians and these were inherited by the Greeks, who gave the science of mathematics its name.

The founder of the first Greek school of mathematics and philosophy was Thales of Miletus, mathematician, merchant, and business tycoon—a good grasp of arithmetic has always been important for trade. He had traveled as a merchant to Egypt, and while there had studied the local geometry and astronomy. His work inspired the breakthroughs made by later Greeks, such as Pythagoras (c. 582–507 B.C.) and Euclid (c. third century B.C.). Another, Edemos, wrote a history of mathematics and claimed that Thales "after a visit to Egypt brought this study to Greece."

Islamic mathematics developed from a deep understanding of Greek works. By the end of the ninth century, the Arabs had translated the mathematical writings of Pythagoras, Archimedes (c. 287–212 B.C.), Ptolemy, and many others. The Arabs were particularly concerned with casting horoscopes through astrological science and the work of mathematicians such as al-Battani (died 929) and Abu' l-Wafa (died 998) made great advances in the geometry used in astronomical calculations. Much of this Arab and Greek learning came to the attention of western Europe by way of Spain, which was under Muslim rule from the eighth century. Muslim power dwindled from the 11th century and in 1185 the university city of Toledo fell into Christian hands, along with its vast library of Arabic and classical texts. Scholarship and mathematics in Western Europe began to be pursued with renewed vigor, in a process that eventually led to the period of great scientific and artistic activity known as the Renaissance.

Among other things, European scholars adopted the Arabic decimal system using nine numerals and a zero, which today is used throughout the world, representing a remarkable form of universal language. However, the name *Arabic* is misleading, for it was probably in India about 2,500 years ago that these numerals were first developed. As with astronomy, India's central position on the Silk and Spice Routes meant that its mathematics was a complex mixture of its own innovations and those it received from abroad. Indian mathematics contributed to both Islamic and Chinese scholarship. Again, its close links with astronomy played a part. In the seventh century, a school was set up in Changan, then the Chinese capital, to study Indian astronomy. During the eighth century, a Chinese astronomer called Qutan Xida translated the Indian calendar under the Chinese title *Jiuzhi Li*, which included discussions of Indian decimal notation and arithmetical rules.

▼ *Bust of the Greek mathematician and philosopher Thales of Miletus (c. 640– 550 B.C.). He is said to have introduced geometry to Greece from Egypt.*

Alchemy and Chemistry

Although chemistry as we know it today really only began in the second half of the 18th century, many processes that have been practiced for thousands of years involve chemical changes. Among them are dyeing materials, tanning leather, smelting metals, glazing pottery, and making glass. Knowledge of chemical processes was therefore well advanced long before the chemical revolution of the 18th century.

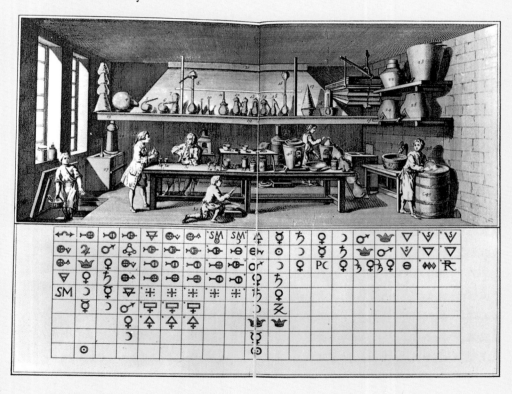

► *Late 18th-century engraving showing a European laboratory. Many of the instruments used in chemical experiments can be seen. The table of chemical symbols below is still based on those used in alchemy, indicating the close links between the two sciences.*

Chemistry, the study of the substances that make up the world around us, also has its origins in the ancient practice of alchemy, as well as in industrial processes. The very word *chemistry* comes from the Arabic *al quemia*, meaning "alchemy." Alchemy was an early form of chemistry that began about 2,000 years ago. Alchemists were interested in finding a method of turning ordinary metals, such as iron, into gold. There was often a lot of magic and superstition involved but, although alchemy is not considered a real science now, a number of scientific methods were used by alchemists and they made some important discoveries.

Over the centuries, the Chinese, in particular a religious group called the Taoists, acquired a huge amount of chemical knowledge and made a number of valuable contributions to the subject. Their main aim in alchemy was to find the secret of immortality, a means to arrest the aging process. Although this eluded them, in seeking it they built up a large body of chemical knowledge, probably including the discovery of gunpowder. This knowledge was gradually transmitted westward in the hands of Indian and Arab scholars, but a great deal of information reached Europe in the 17th century through Jesuit missionaries (see page 25).

Alchemy was practiced in India much later than in other areas, and it was probably imported from China with the spread of Buddhism. Islamic alchemy, which raised the subject to new heights of sophistication, may also have derived from Chinese sources. Alchemical studies were very important in Islamic thinking, and although they used magic and spells they also involved the use of experiment. This laid the foundations of several modern sciences including chemistry and mineralogy (the study of minerals), an important legacy of Islamic culture to the West.

Islam was also heir to the whole Hellenistic Greek alchemical heritage of Alexandria, a major center of Greek learning, and Muslim sources contain the names of nearly all the known Alexandrian alchemists. With their conquests east and west, the Muslims also inherited a huge amount of literature on mineralogy and related fields from the Persians and Indians. Famous names in Islamic alchemy and mineralogy include Ibn Sina (980–1037), known in the West as Avicenna, and Abu Rayhan al-Biruni (937–c. 1050). As with other sciences, this knowledge filtered through to European scholars through Muslim Spain and the Byzantine Empire. Arab trading contacts with Venice and Genoa also contributed to the process as did the more violent contact of the Crusades from the 11th to 13th centuries.

▼ *Engraving of an alchemist in the 17th century. One of the aims of the alchemist was to turn base metals into gold and his experiments were often surrounded by secrecy and magic.*

▶ *An alchemist at work in the Middle East today. He still uses a number of the old instruments, such as the alembic shown here, similar to those used in the engraving (above right).*

Health and Medicine

▲ *Bust of Hippocrates of Cos (c. 450–370 B.C.), the "father of medicine." He believed that diet and hygiene were important in building up a patient's strength.*

▼ *A scene from a 13th-century Italian manuscript by Roger of Salerno. The writer was clearly influenced by Muslim medical practices.*

Chemistry and alchemy also have their roots in the making of drugs for medicine. Throughout history, people have always had to deal with disease, illness, and death, although diagnosis and treatments have varied from region to region. In many places, illness was seen either as an invasion of the body by some poison or it was attributed to the work of an angry god, malignant magic, or witchcraft. Early physicians therefore needed to be part doctor and part priest, for while they believed that medical treatment could relieve a sickness, the main cause could only be removed with prayers and sacrifices to the gods.

The best-known ancient Indian medical text is the *Ayurveda*. This was a compendium of medical practice and was compiled about 700 B.C. In it, disease is seen as an imbalance of substances in the body. Doctors used medicines to drive out harmful substances and replace them with good ones. They were skilled surgeons. The *Ayurveda* also shows that Indian doctors had a thorough understanding of the human diet and the digestive system. The text describes many different types of surgical operations, especially on the stomach and bladder, and even to remove cataracts from eyes.

Many concepts of Greek medicine were borrowed from the Indians: From early times, they were probably imported through trade contacts and later via the Asian conquests of Alexander the Great. Alexander's army physicians, for example, did not know of any cures for snakebites and other diseases endemic to the area. Indian doctors were called in to help and some of them later accompanied the army when it returned to Greece, bringing with them their skills.

Much earlier, in the fifth century B.C., a medical school on the small Greek island of Cos became very influential. This was the home of Hippocrates (c. 450–370 B.C.), often known as the "father of medicine." Like modern doctors, he insisted on keeping medical

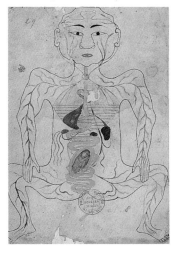

records, noting when treatments failed as well as when they succeeded. Greek medicine, passed on by the Muslims, was very influential in Medieval and Renaissance Europe. Even today, in many parts of the world doctors make a promise to work for the benefit of the patient at all times. This is known as the Hippocratic Oath.

In biology and medical sciences, Islam inherited a vast amount of material from the Greeks, Romans, Persians, and Indians. The result of this amalgamation was the creation of an extensive field embracing nearly every branch of the medical sciences. In particular, Islamic medicine owed much to the work of the Graeco-Roman doctor named Galen (c. A.D. 129–200). His works were among the first Greek texts to be translated into Arabic. By the late ninth century, Islamic medicine was making great advances of its own. One of the most important physicians of this period was Abu Bakr al-Razi (c. 854–c. 930), known in the Medieval West as Rhazes. Ibn Sina also contributed to medicine when he wrote the *Canon*, a huge book that influenced teaching in Europe until the 17th century.

◀ *Illustration from a 13th-century Arabic treatise on medicine. It depicts two doctors mixing ingredients to make a medicine. Plants as well as chemicals were used in the mixtures.*

▼ *Diagram of a pregnant woman, taken from an 11th-century Arabic work on anatomy by Mansour ibn-Ahmed. Arab physicians and doctors made considerable advances in the study of anatomy.*

▼ *View of the Osmania Hospital in southern Pakistan, built by the nizam of Hyderabad in the 19th century. Some of the first public hospitals, where doctors were trained and patients treated, were built in the Muslim world.*

The Shift from East to West

▲ *Mid-19th-century Chinese painting of European passengers disembarking from a British ship, which combines sail, steam, and paddle power.*

▼ *Part of the Great Exhibition held in the Crystal Palace in London in 1851. Although displaying goods from all over the world, this exhibition clearly showed the superiority of Western technology in the 19th century.*

With the decline of Roman power, western Europe had become something of a backwater and there was a general stagnation in its technology, arts, and scholarship. Byzantium continued in the Graeco-Roman tradition, but from the seventh century the rise of the Arab Empire, and the extraordinary flowering of the Islamic culture that followed, eclipsed Byzantium's ancient glory. As we have seen in this book, for nearly a thousand years the flow of ideas in technology and science was largely from Asia into Europe.

Gradually, the balance began to change. Profiting from the learning of Asia and Byzantium, western Europe began to emerge from its "Dark Ages." From the medieval period (c. 1000) through to the

◀ *View of a European iron foundry c. 1900. The development of new processes in iron production laid the foundations for the Industrial Revolution that was to transform Europe from an agricultural society to an industrial one.*

Renaissance, more European cities became actively involved in trade, generating the wealth to finance new universities and places of learning. Increasing European naval expertise led to discoveries from the 15th century that opened up still further possibilities for trade—a route to India around Africa, bypassing the Middle East, and even of a "New World," America. By the start of the 18th century, Europe's command of the seas had led to its increasing domination of the world's trade markets and the slow erosion of the ancient trade patterns of the Silk and Spice Routes.

It was from this strong position, and no doubt partly because of it, that from the mid-1700s the so-called Industrial Revolution began in Europe, transforming its economy from one based on agriculture to one centered on ever-expanding industrial cities. In little more than a century, the revolution in Europe was largely complete, with the United States not far behind. The European and American output of trade goods entirely outstripped that of Asia, swamping their markets. The Indian textile industry collapsed, for example, unable to compete with the steam-driven looms of Europe.

China and Japan were the two nations to resist most determinedly the onslaught of European traders. It was not until 1842 and 1854 respectively that they were finally forced to open their ports to foreign trade. Both received a vast influx of European goods, but also increased the possibilities for their export trade. The Japanese, in particular, embraced Western technology and science, and went out of their way to modernize and industrialize in a plan to make their country as rich and influential as the Western powers. The first railroad in Japan was opened in 1872, only 47 years after the opening in England of the first railroad of all. In much the same way that Europe had adopted and developed the technology and science of Asia during the Renaissance, the way was now open for Asian countries to do the same with the technology of the West.

▲ *Pottery models of European merchants, made in China c. 1730. This type of figure was made as a souvenir and taken home by the merchants and sailors.*

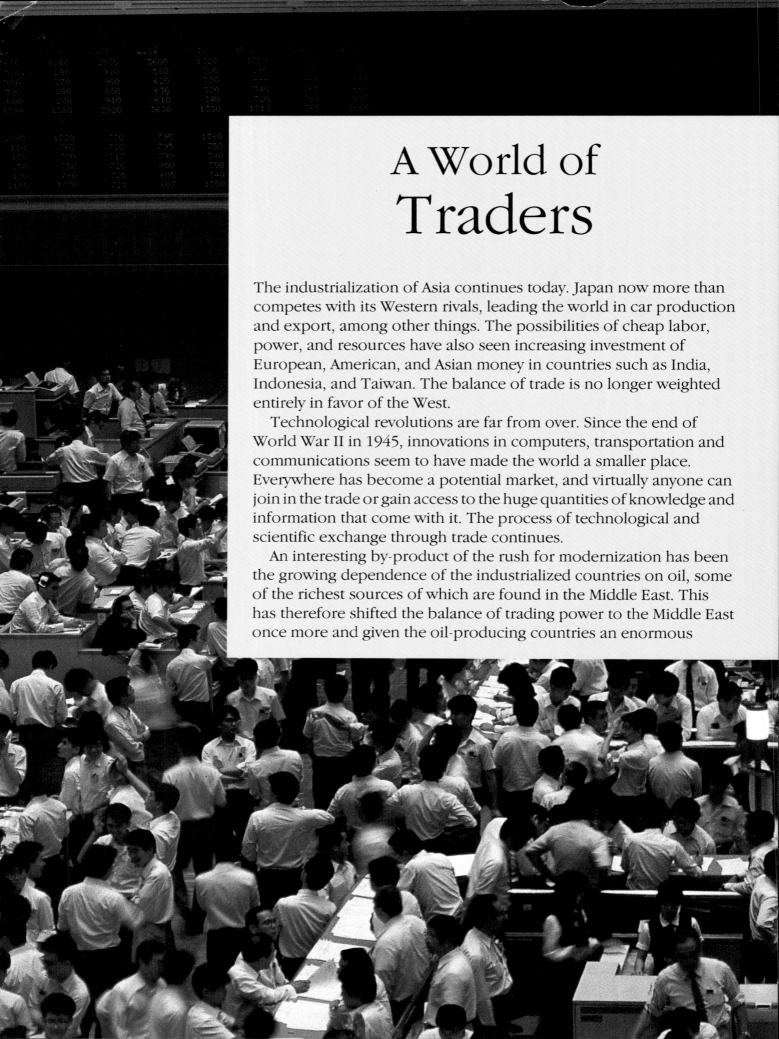

A World of Traders

The industrialization of Asia continues today. Japan now more than competes with its Western rivals, leading the world in car production and export, among other things. The possibilities of cheap labor, power, and resources have also seen increasing investment of European, American, and Asian money in countries such as India, Indonesia, and Taiwan. The balance of trade is no longer weighted entirely in favor of the West.

Technological revolutions are far from over. Since the end of World War II in 1945, innovations in computers, transportation and communications seem to have made the world a smaller place. Everywhere has become a potential market, and virtually anyone can join in the trade or gain access to the huge quantities of knowledge and information that come with it. The process of technological and scientific exchange through trade continues.

An interesting by-product of the rush for modernization has been the growing dependence of the industrialized countries on oil, some of the richest sources of which are found in the Middle East. This has therefore shifted the balance of trading power to the Middle East once more and given the oil-producing countries an enormous influence over the world's economy. This power was seen in 1974, when the oil-producing countries suddenly doubled the price of oil, and in the Persian Gulf War of 1991.

Despite industrialization, the old patterns of trade have not completely disappeared. Arab dhows and Chinese junks still sail the Spice Routes, trading on a small scale from port to port, while camel caravans still carry goods across the deserts. Markets and bazaars take place in virtually every town and city along the ancient Silk Route, providing a place to sell local produce or cheap, mass-produced goods, from pots and pans to trinkets and T-shirts. Most of the carpets these markets sell are factory-made, although carpets are still woven in homes and villages across Asia, but, more often than not, these are exported to the more lucrative markets of the West. The small-scale traders who make a living in this way must constantly battle to survive against the inroads of multinational companies. Today, many of the poorer countries through which the ancient Silk and Spice Routes pass are looking for ways to preserve their old traditions – a difficult task in the economic realities of today's world.

▼ The stock exchange in Tokyo, Japan. Thousands of people congregate here every day to trade on the international markets of stocks and shares, making and losing large sums of money with no physical exchange of goods at all.

▶ Ancient trading patterns have not been completely overwhelmed by technological advances. Here, ironically, a camel is used to transport a motorcycle to its buyer in the Silk Route city of Turfan.

A Silk and Spice Routes Time Chart

Date	Europe	Middle East & central Asia	China & the Far East
3000– 0 B.C.	**c.3000** *Minoan civilization, the earliest in Europe, develops in Crete.* **c.1000–800** *Greek-speaking peoples move into Greece and begin to trade by sea throughout the Mediterranean. Egyptian and Middle East knowledge begins to be acquired.* **753** *Rome founded.* **c.450** *Athens emerges as the strongest city-state in Greece.* **336-323** *Empire of Alexander the Great. Takes Greek knowledge and learning into Asia.* **c.250** *Roman expansion begins.* **146** *Greece comes under Roman rule.*	**c.3000** *Domestication of the horse.* **c.3000** *Sumerians develop first writing system.* **c.2000** *Domestication of the camel.* **c.1000** *Phoenician alphabet develops.* **c.700** *Lydians introduce coinage.* **c.500** *"Arabic" numeral system developed by Indian scholars.* **550-330** *Achaemenid Empire of Persia. Dynasty falls to Alexander.* **c.450** *Babylonians use mathematics to predict planetary movement.* **247** *Parthians control Persia.* **c.50** *Technique of blowing glass discovered in Roman Syria.*	**c.3000** *Silk first produced in China.* **c.2205-1766** *Xia dynasty in China. First use of written symbols.* **c.1766-1027** *Shang dynasty in China.* **c.1400** *Spinning wheel probably in use for the production of silk.* **1027-221** *Zhou dynasty in China.* **221-206** *Qin dynasty unites whole of China for first time.* **202** *Han dynasty founded.* **c.200** *Paper first made in China.* **c.100** *Han Empire expands in Tarim region of Central Asia. Enables Silk Route to operate right across Asia, connecting China with the West.*
A.D. 1– 500	**c. A.D. 1** *Roman glass industry develops.* **117** *Roman Empire at its largest; a major market for Eastern goods.* **310-337** *Reign of Emperor Constantine. Constantinople replaces Rome as capital of his empire.* **395** *Roman Empire splits into two.* **476** *Western Roman Empire collapses.* **486** *Frankish kingdom formed.*	**c. A.D. 70-224** *Kushan Empire of Central Asia. Sogdians trading on Silk Route.* **c.200** *Silk is woven into cloth across Asia but using Chinese thread.* **224** *Sasanians seize power from Parthians. Their rule to see advances in production of trade goods.* **c.400** *Silkworms farmed in Central Asia.*	**c. A.D. 100** *Buddhism reaches China. Contact with Indian knowledge.* **220** *Han dynasty ends. China fragments until reunited by Sui in 589.* **300s** *Secrets of sericulture begin to spread west along the Silk Route.* **400s** *Improved techniques in glass production introduced to the Chinese by the Sogdians.*
501– 1000	**500s** *Stirrup first used in Europe.* **c.552** *Silkworms farmed in Europe.* **610** *Remains of Roman Empire now known as Byzantine Empire.* **c.700** *Lateen sail introduced to Mediterranean from Indian Ocean.* **711** *Arab conquest of Spain. Will lead to introduction of much Eastern technology and science to Europe.* **800s** *Venice formed as a city-state.*	**500s** *Turks establish empire across northern Asia, taking in Sogdian territories. Sogdians still trade.* **632** *Muslim Arab expansion begins.* **651** *Sasanians fall to the Arabs. Islamic technology develops with Sasanian and Byzantine influences.* **751** *Arabs defeat Chinese in Central Asia. Capture Chinese papermakers.* **mid-900s** *Muslim Empire fragments.*	**618-907** *Tang dynasty rules in China. Open to foreign influences, e.g. Indian mathematics is taught.* **700s** *Block printing in China.* **800s** *First porcelain made in China. Gunpowder invented.* **c.850** *Compass begins to be used by Chinese for navigational purposes.* **919** *First use of gunpowder in battle.* **976** *Song dynasty controls China.*
1001– 1400	**1001** *Start of Medieval Period.* **1096-1291** *Period of Crusades. General exchange of technology between Europe and Middle East.* **c.1200** *Compass used by Europeans.* **1236** *Mongols invade Russia.* **1265** *Gunpowder recorded in Europe.* **1300s** *Paper made across Europe.* **1338** *Spinning wheel in Europe.* **1346** *Battle of Crécy between French and English. First European use of cannons.*	**c.1200** *Arab and Persian sailors using navigational compass.* **1260-1368** *Mongols control Central and much of Western Asia. Silk Route prospers under Pax Mongolica. Period of major technological exchange across Asia and into Europe.* **1281-1326** *Reign of Osman I, founder of Turkish Ottoman empire.* **c.1300** *Movable type in use in Central Asia.*	**c.1001** *Paper banknotes in China.* **c.1050** *Movable type in China.* **1126** *China divided into two.* **1196** *Ghengis Khans unites Mongols. Expansion of Mongol Empire begins.* **1264** *Kublai Khan founds Mongol Yuan dynasty in China.* **1288** *Bronze handgun, the earliest known, made in China.* **1368** *Yuan dynasty overthrown by the Ming dynasty. Foreign influences discouraged in China.*
1401– 1750	**c.1401** *Renaissance period begins.* **1453** *Constantinople falls to Ottoman Turks. Byzantine Empire collapses.* **1455** *Gutenberg printing press in use.* **1492** *All Muslim power in Spain over.* **1497-1499** *Vasco da Gama sails from Portugal via Africa to India.* **c.1650** *Agricultural Revolution begins.* **c.1750** *Industrial Revolution begins.*	**1405** *Final collapse of Mongols. Silk Route no longer a major trade link.* **1500s** *Decline of routes linking Indian Ocean with Mediterranean as Europe trades with Asia via Africa.* **1526-1857** *Muslim Mogul dynasty of India. Encourages European trade.* **1594** *English first trade with India, the start of their increasing power there.*	**1405-1433** *Chinese explore the Spice Routes as far as Africa.* **1511** *Portuguese take Melaka.* **1570-1637** *Japan open to foreign traders but closes again until 1853.* **1596** *Dutch arrive in East Indies.* **1600s** *Jesuits in China.* **1644-1912** *Qing dynasty rules China. Limited foreign trade until 1842.*

Glossary

alchemy: the search for the technique of changing base metals, such as iron and lead, into silver and gold. It is often associated with magic. However, alchemy was often extended into wider areas of study, laying the foundations of the science of chemistry.

astrology: the study of the positions of the planets and stars in the belief that they influence events on earth. Today, it is not generally accepted as scientifically accurate, but it has attracted serious scientific study over the centuries.

astronomy: one of the oldest of the sciences, astronomy involves the study of the sun, moon, stars and planets and all other objects in the universe. It is concerned with their positions, movements, and their origins and evolution.

Avars: a Central Asian nomadic people who invaded the area of Russia north of the Black Sea in the 6th century A.D., establishing control over a large area of land. Their power was limited after defeat by the Emperor Charlemagne in 796.

Babylonians: a people who ruled from their capital at Babylon in Mesopotamia (present-day Iraq) from about 2000 B.C. They were heavily influenced by Sumerian culture. The Babylonian Empire was taken into the Persian Empire in 539 B.C.

Buddhism: a religious path taught in India by Siddhartha Gautama (c. 560-486 B.C.), known as the Buddha. It declares that by understanding the origins of all human suffering, people can reach perfect enlightenment or nirvana.

Byzantium: the original name for Constantinople (now Istanbul), the capital of the Eastern Roman Empire. The empire became known as the Byzantine Empire (610-1453 A.D.) and is often simply referred to as Byzantium.

caliph: the title of the successors of Muhammad as rulers in the Islamic world. At first the caliph was elected but later the office became hereditary.

caravansaries: a large inn enclosing a courtyard providing shelter and accommodation for caravans of travellers and their camels or other pack animals.

Christianity: the religion founded in Palestine by the followers of Jesus of Nazareth (c. 5 B.C.-A.D. 29), later known as Jesus Christ. His teachings spread rapidly throughout the Roman Empire until Christianity became the official state religion toward the end of the 4th century A.D.

colonize: to establish a colony in an area. A colony is a settlement of people in a foreign country who maintain close ties with their homeland. A colonial empire is subject territory occupied by settlers from the ruling state.

Crusades: a series of wars over the years 1096-1291 waged by the Christian European rulers to recapture Palestine (the Holy Land) from the Muslims. The desire for land and trade soon took over from the original religious motivation.

Franciscans: a Christian order of friars founded in 1209 by St. Francis of Assisi (1182-1226). He lived a life of poverty and service while preaching a simple form of the Christian gospel.

Gutenberg, Johann: German printer (c. 1397-1468) who designed and built the first European printing press. This used movable type and by 1500 this method of printing had spread through much of Europe.

irrigation: bringing water along specially built channels onto dry land so crops can be grown there.

Islam: this means literally "surrender" (to God). Islam is the religion founded by Muhammad (c. A.D. 570-632) whose followers became known as Muslims. The Koran is Islam's sacred scripture that teaches that there is only one God and that Muhammad is His prophet.

Jesuits: members of the largest and most influential Roman Catholic religious order (also known as the Society of Jesus) founded in 1534 by St. Ignatius Loyola (1491-1556). The aim of the order was to protect Catholicism against the Protestant Reformation and to carry out missionary work. The Jesuits have a tradition of learning and science.

Lydians: a people of the ancient kingdom of Lydia (7th to 6th centuries B.C.) in Anatolia (now part of Turkey), with its capital at Sardis. Their last king, Croesus, was defeated by the Persians in 546 B.C.

Marco Polo: A Venetian merchant (1254-1324) famous for his account of his travels in Asia. After traveling overland to China (1271-1275) with his father and uncle, he spent 17 years serving the Mongol emperor of China, Kublai Khan, before returning to Venice by sea (1292-1295).

metallic luster: a shiny metallic surface found on some pottery and porcelain. It is achieved by using metallic paints under the glaze.

Muslim: see *Islam.*

Nestorianism: a belief held by Nestorius (died c. 457), the Christian patriarch of Constantinople, that Jesus was two persons, one human and one divine. The orthodox view is that his dual nature was contained within one body, so Nestorius's belief was declared heretical. Nestorius was exiled and subsequent persecution led to a wide dispersal of his followers.

Phoenicians: an ancient people of skilled sailors and great merchants. From about 1100 B.C. they lived in cities such as Sidon and Tyre along the eastern coast of the Mediterranean Sea in the area now known as Lebanon.

porcelain: a very fine ceramic or pottery ware. It is sometimes known as china, as it was the Chinese who developed the technique of making porcelain some time before A.D. 900.

Sasanians: the ruling people of Iran from A.D. 224, after their defeat of the Parthians. Over the next 400 years, the Sasanians controlled Persia (Iran) and other areas of Western Asia, until they in turn fell before the Arab armies in A.D. 642.

Scythians: a nomadic people who occupied a region to the north of the Black Sea around the 8th to 4th centuries B.C. They are famous for their ornaments of gold and electrum (a natural alloy of gold and silver) with animal decoration.

silk: the very fine fiber produced by the silk moth caterpillar when it makes its cocoon. Silken twine is made from the fibers and this can be woven to make fabrics. The craft of producing silk and its cloth is known as sericulture.

smelt: to extract a metal from an ore by heating.

Sogdians: a people who occupied the region of Central Asia around the modern city of Samarkand. Because of their strategic position on the main east-west trade routes, they formed an important link in the chain of cultural exchange from around the 1st century A.D. Sogdiana remained a prosperous center until the Mongol invasions.

Sumerians: a people from the area between the Tigris and Euphrates rivers in lower Mesopotamia (present-day Iraq) who developed what is probably the earliest civilization. From about 3500 B.C. they had writing, trade, planned cities with public buildings, and irrigation systems.

Turks: natives of Turkey, but the name is also applied to Turkic speaking people as a whole. The Turks originated in Central Asia but pushed westward into Byzantine territories during the 15th century. They established their own empire, known as the Ottoman Empire (after the ruling Ottoman dynasty) throughout the Middle East and Balkan region of Europe.

Index

Bold numerals indicate an illustration or map.

First American publication 1994 by New Discovery Books, Macmillan Publishing Company, 866 Third Avenue, New York, NY 10022, USA
Macmillan Publishing Company is part of the Maxwell Communication Group of Companies.
Library of Congress Cataloging-in-Publication Data
Reid, Struan
    Inventions and trade/Struan Reid
        p. cm.   (The silk and spice routes)
    Includes index.
    ISBN 0-02-726316-9
    1. Technological innovations—Economic aspects—History—Juvenile literature. 2. Economic history—Juvenile literature. 3. Inventions—History—Juvenile literature. 4. Commerce—History—Juvenile literature. 5. Silk Road—History—Juvenile literature. 6. Trade routes—History—Juvenile literature.
    [1. Technological innovations. 2. Inventions—History. 3. Commerce—History. 4. Silk Road—History. 5. Trade routes—History.] I. Title. II. Series.
HC79.T4R44 1995 382'.09—dc20   93-41629
Summary: Describes how discoveries and commerce helped to open up the Silk and Spice Routes to European exploration.
First published in Great Britain in 1994 by
Belitha Press Limited, 31 Newington Green, London N16 9PU
Printed in China for Imago
Specialist Consultants: Dr. André Singer, Professor Denis Simon and Mr. Samin Amin

Acknowledgments

Ancient Art and Architecture Collection title page, 9, 10 top, 16 left, 17 top, 40 top; Archiv fur Kunst und Geschichte, Berlin 25 top (Bibliotèque Nationale, Paris), 29 centre and 32 centre right (Free Library, Philadelphia), 41 top (Osterreichisches Nationalbibliothek, Vienna); Archivi Alinari 34 top; Bibliothèque Nationale back cover, 12, 14 top, 18 bottom, 24 centre, 41 centre; Bodleian Library, Oxford 15 centre; Bridgeman Art Library 14 bottom (British Library), 37 bottom (Galleria Nazionale delle Marche, Urbino); British Library 30 centre; British Museum 11 left, 19 centre and bottom left, 22 left, 32 top, 33 centre; Devizes Museum 7 top; Douglas Dickins 41 bottom; E.T. Archive 9 inset (Louvre, Paris), 14 centre (Science Museum), 15 top (British Library), 19 bottom right (Naples Museum), 20 bottom and 21 top and centre (Musée Guimet, Paris), 26 top (Museum of Roman Civilisation, Rome), 27 centre (Hermitage, St Petersburg), 36 top (British Museum); Mary Evans Picture Library back cover, 16 right, 18 top, 26 centre left and centre right, 32 centre left, 37 centre, 39 centre, 42 top and bottom, 43 top; Robert Harding Picture Library front cover bottom, 6 centre and bottom, 7 top, 13 bottom, 17 centre, 21 bottom, 23 left, 27 bottom, 28 centre left, 35 centre, 36 centre; Roland and Sabrina Michaud from The John Hillelson Agency front cover top, 25 bottom left, 31, 34 bottom, 39 bottom; Image Bank, London 45 inset; Image Select 28 top; Impact Photos 44-45 (Julian Calder); Kunsthistorisches Museum, Vienna 8 top; Magnum Photos 23 bottom (Erich Lessing); Toby Molenaar 10 bottom; National Museum of Ireland, Dublin 8 bottom; RMN 29 top (Louvre, Paris); Royal Astronomical Society, London 35 bottom; Scala 20 centre; State Hermitage Museum, St Petersburg, Russia 28 centre right; Sultanate of Oman 13 top (Mohammed Mustafa); Topkapi Palace Museum 12 left, 22 right, 23 top right; Trinity College, Cambridge 40 bottom; UNESCO/Silk Roads Photograph donated by the photographer to the 'Intergral Study of the Silk Roads: Roads of Dialogue' 11 right (Toby Molenaar), 30 top and 33 top (Anne Garde), 33 bottom (Liu Weinmin); courtesy of the Trustees of the V & A 20 top; Werner Archive 43 centre and bottom (Handels-og-Sofarts Museum, Slot Kronborg).